Buck Wilder's™ Adventures

Book #3

THE ANTS DIG TO CHINA

Mackinac

for the love of reading

Other Buck Wilder Books

Buck Wilder's Adventures
#1 Who Stole the Animal Poop?
#2 The Work Bees Go on Strike
#3 The Ants Dig to China

Buck Wilder's Animal Wisdom
Buck Wilder's Small Fry Fishing Guide
Buck Wilder's Small Twig Hiking and Camping Guide
Buck Wilder's Little Skipper Boating Guide

...and more to come...

#4 The Owls Don't Give a Hoot
#5 The Salmon Stop Running
#6 The Squirrels Go Nuts

Buck Wilder's Animal Adventures #3: The Ants Dig to China
Written by Timothy R. Smith

Copyright 2007 Timothy R. Smith

Library of Congress Cataloging-in-Publication Data

Smith, Timothy R.

Buck Wilder's Adventures #3
The Ants Dig to China
Summary: Buck Wilder and friends work to solve why there is a large ant hill blocking the animal expressway.

ISBN 1-934133-07-8
ISBN13 978-1934133-07-1

Fiction
10 9 8 7 6 5 4 3

A Mackinac Island Press, Inc. publication
Traverse City, Michigan

www.mackinacislandpress.com

Printed in the United States

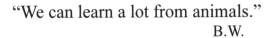

"We can learn a lot from animals."
B.W.

THE ANTS
DIG TO CHINA

CHAPTERS

INTRODUCTION

In case you haven't read Buck Wilder's first two adventure stories, Who Stole the Animal Poop? and The Work Bees Go on Strike, you will need to know who Buck Wilder is. You also should know where he lives and why he lives there, who his friends are, and why so many of the animals come to visit him.

First, you will have to see his home. Hidden way back in the woods, deep in the forest, where only the animal trails go, beyond the pond and over the stream, is a very big wooden house. It has doors, windows, decks, a fireplace, and most of the things a big log cabin in the woods would have. The only thing different about this house is that it is built in the trees. It is a giant tree house and you can only reach it by ladder.

In this tree house lives a very interesting and smart man. His name is Buck Wilder. He is a little older, has a beard, wears glasses, and you rarely see him without his hat on. He is good, honest, and can always be trusted. Trust is something you always want to have with a friend.

He shares what he has and the animals know it. He lives in the woods because he loves nature. He loves to be among the trees, the plants, the flowers, the animals, the insects–everything that lives in the woods. He learns from nature and understands how it is all connected. There is no TV in Buck's house. His entertainment comes from outside his windows and there is always some kind of entertainment going on. Nature never stops and he loves to be part of it. Buck Wilder looks kind of like this:

Buck has a bunch of animal friends that live in the woods surrounding his big tree house. They respect Buck for his common sense and his ability to think things out—something the animals have a problem doing. Buck doesn't have all the answers, but he can help you figure out the problem or the dilemma. And in the woods, among the animals, there always seems to be some kind of problem or dilemma. The animals don't just visit Buck when there is a problem. They like him a lot. They like to visit, tell stories, and see if there's any extra food in his refrigerator. Normally there is and Buck is always there to share with a big smile

Buck's animal friends look a
little like this:

Buck's best friend is Rascal Raccoon who lives with Buck in his tree house. They have been friends for a long time. When Rascal is not outside climbing trees or chasing squirrels, which he does just for fun because he's a rascal, you will find him taking long naps on one of Buck's fluffy rugs. Most of the time he likes to sleep on the rug next to the fish tank just so he can keep an eye on the fish. He loves to play the catch and release game with the fish.

Rascal looks something like this:

This is a story about a problem the animals were having in the woods and how they came to Buck for help. It is a good story because it is a Buck Wilder Adventure story–and here it comes! It's the story about what happened when the ants decided to

    dig

      a

        hole

          straight

            through

              to

                China!

TURN THE PAGE
and
let's get started

CHAPTER 1

IT STARTED LIKE THIS

It had been a regular day for Buck. He started the day with a strong cup of coffee, a bowl of cereal with some wild strawberries and fresh milk, and some morning exercise of chopping wood. Splitting wood not only loosened Buck up a little for the day and gave him a little exercise, it also helped to build the winter wood supply for the fireplace.

Sometimes, for hours, Buck would just swing that axe and split piles of wood. It gave him a sense of accomplishment. He was never afraid of hard work.

Rascal would usually just stay out of the way, avoiding the flying woodchips. He might wander off into the woods to meet his animal friends or go play by the stream. The stream is where Rascal also likes to take a bath.

In many ways animals are a lot like people. If they don't take baths or wash themselves they will start to stink—and nobody likes to be around anything that stinks!

So everyone, including the animals, need to hit that water as often as they can and scrub down.

During the afternoon, when Rascal returned to take a nap and Buck came inside to make some sandwiches for lunch, the bell rang.

When the bell rings it means a visitor has come to Buck's house and the ladder needs to be lowered to let them in.

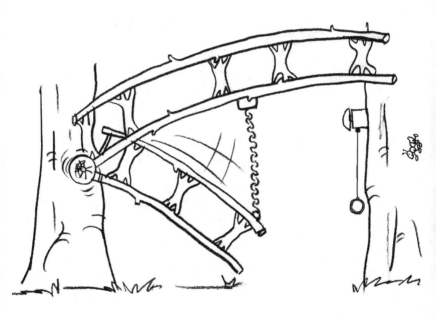

CHAPTER 2

MAURY'S DILEMMA

"Hello down there," hollered Rascal. "Who is it?"

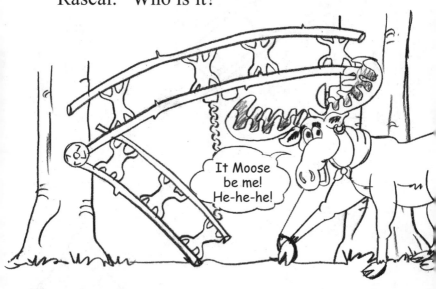

"It's me, Maury the Moose. Can you let down the ladder so I can come up and visit?"

"It's coming down," called Rascal and down came the ladder. One of Rascal's chores was to lower the ladder.

Clip-it-ee clop, Clip-it-ee clop, came the familiar sound of Maury the Moose's big feet clanking on the ladder steps.

"Wow, that was a tight fit," said Maury. "My antlers are getting so big I can hardly make it through the hallway. I actually have to tilt them a little to the side or I'll knock a picture off the wall!"

When Maury came down the hall,

Buck knew right away that something wasn't right with Maury. He was usually very cheerful, humming some kind of a tune or getting ready to tell one of his corny jokes. His jokes were always so silly and he would most often start laughing so hard at himself that he rarely finished the joke. That is

what made them so silly. This time was different. Maury was hunched over and he was looking down. He was not the happy moose that he usually was.

"Hey Maury! I am glad you're here. I was just getting ready for lunch. Would you like a twig sandwich? I just cut a bunch of wood this morning. The leaves and branches are really fresh. Maybe a bowl of juicy strawberries and milk?"

"Thanks, Buck. You are a very good host," replied Maury. "Most times I would gobble 'em up in a minute or two, but not today. I have lost my appetite."

"Not feeling well, Maury? You look kind of down and out. Coming

down with the flu or something?" Buck
asked.

"No, Buck, nothing like that. I
do have a problem and I'm hoping you
might be of some help."

"Maury, anytime I can help, just ask. What's up?" Buck asked.

Rascal moved up to the counter to listen a little closer. "Ah, excuse me. If no one wants those strawberries, I'd be glad to digest them," Rascal offered.

"Go right ahead, Rascal," replied Buck. "Eat all you want."

Rascal sat up to the bowl and quietly started to eat them, one at a time. "Yummm," Rascal said.

"Maury, what is the problem? What has gotten you so upset?" Buck asked again.

CHAPTER 3

THE ANIMAL EXPRESSWAY

"Buck, you know my mother Milda?" Maury asked.

"Sure do, Maury. I have known Milda the Moose a long time. She is a great moose," replied Buck.

"Do you know where she lives on the other side of the woods by the beaver pond?"

"Yup," answered Buck.

"It's an out of the way place with not much going on. It is a good place for her to live," Maury said. "She can take care of it easily."

"Yup, I know," replied Buck again.

"Well," continued Maury, "she relies on me to help her out with stuff. Being older she doesn't get out as much and she appreciates it when I bring her some fresh branches and leaves, or some apples, or even turnips when I can find them. Well, the problem I'm having is keeping me away from seeing my mom. I am afraid she is going to get worried and will come looking for me. It isn't safe for an older moose to wander about the forest. There are wolves out there!

I don't want her to get hurt. She's my mom!"

"I understand," said Buck. "I have a mother like that, too. Why can't you get there?"

"Buck, the trail to her house is blocked. Right smack in the middle of the trail to her house is a giant pile of dirt. I mean…it's gigantic! It looks like an Egyptian pyramid of dirt and it is right in the middle of the forest, right where all the main animal trails cross.

34

"It is blocking everything…and it's new. It wasn't there last month, and it seems to be getting bigger every day. I can't get over it or around it. I am proud of how big I am and how big my antlers are. Most animals envy their size, but if I get off a main trail I am in trouble because my antlers run into all those low hanging tree limbs and bushes. I can't get anywhere. I get stuck. I need the main trail to my mom's. Buck, I would appreciate any help you can give me."

"Maury, you have been a friend for a long time and I like your mom a lot too. It would be my honor to help you. Let's see what we can do," Buck said. "Rascal, would you please go with

Maury and find out what is going on. What is this thing blocking the trail system? Why is it there? What is it and how can we get through it or around it? Rascal, my little detective friend, let me know what you find out."

"Thanks for your time, Buck. I really appreciate your help. Let's go, Rascal," said Maury, and off they went.

CHAPTER 4

CHECK IT OUT!

Rascal and Maury went down the trail that led from Buck's house, crossed over the stream (which is Buck's favorite fishing spot), and headed to the center of the woods. On the way Rascal turned to Maury and said, "Maury, do you remember when we staked out the beehive and I sat up in your antlers all night?"

"Sure do," replied Maury. "We discovered who was taking more than their fair share and we helped solve the honey mystery! That was a great time. What great memories!"

"Well, put me up in those antlers again and let's make some new memories," said Rascal as he climbed up into Maury's big antlers.

Then Rascal and Maury continued on the trail. Maury was almost a full-grown male adult moose and was close to 1000 pounds of muscle on four legs. There wasn't anything bigger in the forest and all the animals knew it. Out of pure respect...they would just move aside.

It didn't take long before Rascal and Maury reached one of the main animal trails and saw that the traffic was stopped. Animals were backed up everywhere. Porcupines, opossums, skunks, wild turkeys, and deer all over—just standing there, grunting and groaning. It sounded like they were honking their horns. They weren't moving anywhere and they didn't look very happy.

Maury and Rascal walked up to the closest animal on the trail, Jake Turkey. He was a big ol' gobbler with a long white beard.

41

"Jake, what is going on? Maury tells me the trail is blocked. Is anybody getting through? How long have you been here?" Rascal asked.

"A long time," replied Jake. "I don't like it. My family is getting hungry and we need to get down the trail to the acorn patch or there will be trouble in paradise! And look who is in front of me on the trail–Sylvia Skunk."

"She's got an attitude and I don't know when she'll go off!" Jake continued. "Of all the animals in the woods, I don't want to be around her when she decides to let loose. Sylvia has quite a bad temper and if she decides to let loose we will have to jump in the stream to take a bath. Things are a little touchy along this trail. We know there is something blocking the trail and there are all kinds of rumors as to why–a deer ran into a moose, the swamp mosquitoes are on attack, the ants have built a blockade…I don't care what it is but we have to get moving. We are hungry!"

CHAPTER 5

DIAMOND DEELORES

Just then Rascal heard one of his favorite bird friends making her favorite woodsy call, "chic-a-dee, chic-a-dee-dee."

"Hey Deelores. Is that you?"

"Sure is, Rascal," responded Deelores as she came in closer. Deelores's nickname is Dee. She likes to call her own name in song. If you ever hear her birdcall stop and listen closely and you will hear Deelores's name, "Chic-a-dee, chic-a-dee-dee, chic-a-dee-dee-dee!" The call comes from a cute little black and white bird, a little smaller than an English sparrow but bigger than a hummingbird. You will see it, usually with others, jumping around small bushes and pine trees just singing away, eating small seeds and berries, and acting like there are no problems in the world. They will make you smile.

Diamonds are a girl's best friend!

"Hey Deelores. I could use your help," said Rascal.

"Hi Rascal. Hi Maury," answered Deelores. "You sure do look big up there in Maury's antlers. Don't fall: it is a long way down."

"I'll be careful. Thanks for the concern," replied Rascal.

"Here is what I need some help with. Our woods are clogged up with animals that can't get down their animal trails. Something big is blocking the way. Do you think you could fly over, take a good look and let me know what you see? It would be a big favor."

"Rascal," replied Deelores, "I've already seen it. All of us that can fly have been over there to check it out.

It is a great big mess. It looks like somebody has dropped a giant load of dirt, mountain sized, right smack in the middle of the woods, right where all the animal trails cross, and it is blocking traffic. Animals are backed up all over the place. Talk about a giant traffic jam! Some are even yelling at each other… it's animal road rage!"

"Deelores, do you have any ideas how it could have gotten there, who did it, or why? Maury said it wasn't here last month."

"I don't know where it came from," responded Deelores, "but I do know it is a strange pile of dirt. It has a hole straight down the middle of it and it's spitting out dirt just like a volcano

spits out lava. The dirt is flying all over the place and it appears the only ones in the forest that can get over that thing are the ants. They seem to be running up and down it on both sides. Ants are always running over everything, everywhere, all the time. What is unusual though is that the ants seem to be talking to each other in some kind of strange gibberish. I couldn't understand them. It almost sounded like Chinese!"

Chapter 6

Thistle Seed

"Hmmmm, that is very interesting. Deelores, would you please do us a favor and fly over to Buck's house to tell him what you saw? I know he will figure it out. Maury and I will be along shortly."

"Maybe I'll get lucky because sometimes he puts thistle seed in his birdfeeder and as a chickadee, I can't

think of anything more delicious to eat than thistle seed. See you there," and off she went.

Needless to say, Deelores was on Buck's birdfeeder a long time before Rascal and Maury made it back down the trail to Buck's house. "This bird seed is so good. I'm stuffed! I don't think I can eat anymore or I'll explode! This feeder is full of thistle seed. Buck is so generous."

Just then the window cracked open and Buck stuck his head out. "Hey, Deelores! I see you found the thistle seed I just put out fresh today. Glad you like it. Tell the rest of your family about it. I have plenty to share."

Buck then looked down and saw Maury coming through the woods with Rascal on his antlers. "Hey, the ladder is down," hollered Buck. "Come on up.

I want to hear about what is going on."

Maury climbed the ladder, clip-it-ee clop, clip-it-ee clop, still holding Rascal in his antlers. He knocked two pictures off the hallway wall while trying to get into Buck's living room.

"Welcome back," said Buck. "You were kind of noisy coming in. Rascal, you could have climbed down from Maury's antlers and made it a little easier for him to get in here. That hallway wasn't built for a 1000 pound moose carrying a raccoon on his antlers," said Buck with a disapproving look on his face.

"Sorry, Buck," said Rascal as he climbed down to the floor. "But riding on Maury's antlers is the ride of a lifetime. It's like being on a nonstop roller coaster ride. I'm sorry, Buck. I'll clean up the hallway—I promise."

"Okay, enough of that," said Buck. "What did you find out about the trail?

Rascal and Maury explained

what they did, what they saw, and what happened. They then asked Deelores to fly inside and tell Buck what she knew.

CHAPTER 7

WHAT TO DO?

"Hmmmm," said Buck as he took in all the information. "Very interesting bunch of facts, but I'm not sure of how to put them all together. Deelores, if what you say is true, and I don't doubt that, and you think that big dirt mountain blocking the trails is a giant ant hill, then the best thing I can do is go talk to the ants; better yet, the head ant,

Queen Sharmain, who is in charge of the whole ant colony. She is the reason most things happen anyway. The place wouldn't run right and would fall apart if she wasn't around. I would just like to meet with her for a few minutes."

Buck thought for a moment, "I have an idea. Maybe she could come over here. Deelores, would you please do me a favor? Will you fly over to the top of the ant hill and ask the ants to pass a message down to Queen Sharmain? Ask her if she would be so kind as to take a few minutes out of her busy day laying eggs and taking care of the nursery to meet with me. I would like to invite her over for lunch. Dee, I think if you offer her a flight on your back she will come. Give it a try!"

"Okay," said Dee, and out the window she flew, straight for the top of the ant hill. "Chic-a-dee, Chic-a-dee-dee," sang Deelores as she flew from tree to tree.

59

CHAPTER 8

QUEEN SHARMAIN

Ants are fascinating little creatures that are very much like bees. Thousands of them live in a large home called a colony. They work together to help the whole colony, and have one queen ant that rules over all. Ants turn over more soil than any other insect. They are the main scavengers of our world, and there are so many of them that their combined weight is close to that of all humans. Their strength is awesome! They can carry something 50 times their weight and run straight up a tree without stopping. That would be like you carrying a grizzly bear and a moose at the same time!

You will see ants running on the sidewalk, getting into your picnic lunches, and invading your kitchen. They are everywhere!

It didn't take long for Deelores to reach the top of the ant hill and to pass her message down through the ants. Ants talk with each other by rubbing their antennas together. It is their way of sending messages—how to find the spilled ice cream or where the peanut butter and jelly sandwich is. Dee's message to the Queen traveled from ant to ant at super fast speed. And back came Queen Sharmain's answer at the same super speed. It said, "Deelores, wait for me. I would love to go on a flight. I will be there right away. I've always dreamed of flying like a

bird and this is my chance. Plus, I get to have one of Buck's home cooked meals. I'm invited for lunch and don't have to raid his kitchen to get it!"

Right away there were thousands of ants running all over the place. It was like someone had just poked a stick in the side of their ant hill. The word was out that their queen was leaving the ant hill! This is highly uncommon!

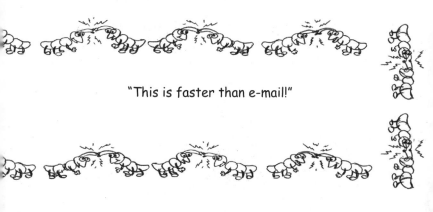

"This is faster than e-mail!"

Out popped Queen Sharmain with a big smile on her face and singing a song. " ♪Fly me to the moon and let me sail among the stars, you can be my Jupiter and I will be your Mars♪." Oh, I am so excited! Let's fly!" Then Queen Sharmain added, "I do have a small favor to ask though. My ant colony is very upset about me leaving my duties, even if it is only for a short time, so they want me to take six ant guards so I return safely. I know you understand."

Chapter 9

The Ride Of A Lifetime

"Of course I understand. Climb on Queen Sharmain, and your guards too. Let's have some fun. Buck is cooking lunch and I'm hoping he is baking some poppy seed rolls. Let's go!" Dee said. Queen Sharmain and her six-armed ant guards climbed on the back of Deelores and off they went. It was the flight of a lifetime. Dee turned in mid-air, glided over the treetops, swooped down over

the lake, and then flew at full speed to Buck's tree house. The ants never stopped talking. "Look at that, look over there—whoops, hold on! Wow!"

Dee flew straight through Buck's window and landed on the kitchen counter. "Hello, Buck," said Queen Sharmain as she climbed off Dee's back. "To fly on a bird's back is one of the most spectacular things I've ever done. Thank you, Dee, and thank you so much, Buck, for arranging it."

The ant guards quickly jumped from Dee's back and stood by the crack of the door, the edge of the window, and any place else they thought needed to be guarded. It is their natural instinct to guard.

"I'm glad you had a good flight," said Buck, "and I'm happy you are here for lunch. I am very honored that you would come to see me. I just baked some fresh poppy seed rolls and, with a little honey or homemade blueberry jam, I guarantee you will never want to leave! Time for lunch."

67

"Just like I told you!" said Dee to Queen Sharmain.

"Oh, are these ever good!" said Queen Sharmain as she buried her face in the honey. "I do love to eat. Guards, come over and grab a bite. It is yummy."

All the ants ate, Rascal licked his fingers, Dee picked the seeds off the bottom of the plate, and Maury just smiled. It was a great lunch.

CHAPTER 10

HOW IT HAPPENED

Queen Sharmain wiped her face clean and said, "We didn't mean to, but I think our giant ant hill has caused a big problem in the woods."

"Yes, it has, Queen Sharmain. Would you mind telling me what it is all about?" asked Buck.

"Yes, I can. It is simple," responded Queen Sharmain. "One day our scout

ants came back from the picnic area over by the corner of the woods where most people go to picnic.

"It is a great place for us to find dropped food. It is generally bits and pieces of the same stuff—potato chips, peanut butter, hot dogs, bread—you know, regular picnic food. Well, this one day our scout ants came back with some food that we had never tried before. It was spicy, tangy, and fun to eat...and I loved it the most! We looked it up on our food chart and found it was Chinese!

FOOD IDENTIFICATION CHART
FOR ANTS

Type of Food	Warnings, Precautions, Pay Attention To	Most Commonly Found in Picnic Areas
Greek	Watch out for what is wrapped in olive leaves. Goat's milk-ug! GREAT HONEY DESSERTS! OUZO tastes like asphalt—"OPA!"	Feta Cheese, Gyros, Musaka, Baklava
Cajun	Can be very spicy—be careful! Rice is dirty. Shrimp and Ochra dishes are the best—"Mon-du-Creole!"	Dirty rice, Gumbo, Jambalaya
Mexican	South of the border foods—tasty! Corn foods, lots of wraps—can be extremely hot-watch out! "ARRIBA-ARRIBA...OLE!"	Tacos, Enchiladas, Nachos, Burritos
Chinese	Lots of soy sauce, spicy and tangy, sweet and sour-tend to overeat. "Ah-so!"	Fried rice, egg rolls, chop suey, chow mein
Sushi	EAT FRESH! After 3 days throw out—just like visiting relatives!	Raw fish rolled up chopped up, but still raw fish!
Italian	Eat only with garlic bread, sing loudly and stay up late. The noodles will stretch. "Buon appetite!"	Pepperoni, Parmesan cheese, Polenta, Spaghetti
German	The strudels are the best. Schnitzel is fun—great sausages. "Vun-de-bar!"	Bratwurst, German Potato Salad, Wiener schnitzel, Dumplings
American	Don't overeat these. High fats and calories-addicting, but tastes great! "Yum!"	Potato Chips, Hot Dogs, Hamburgers, Fries, Fried Chicken, Fudge

"I wanted more…and what the Queen wants, the Queen gets! Since we rarely see Chinese food in the picnic grounds, and my gathering ants didn't know where else to get it, they decided to go to China to get more for me."

Buck and Rascal's faces began to have an astonished look. Dee's eyes opened wider in almost disbelief and Maury's mouth hung open.

Queen Sharmain continued, "Most of my gathering ants thought China was over the next hill or maybe down the road. When we looked on the globe we realized it was on the other side of the world. Knowing that the shortest distance between two points is a straight line, my drilling ants decided to dig a hole straight through to China. So we did."

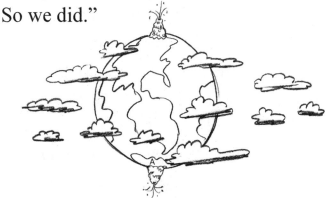

"No way," said Buck with a totally shocked expression on his face.

"Way," said Queen Sharmain. "We dug straight through to China."

Rascal and Dee were so stunned they couldn't talk. Maury's mouth still hung open. Buck then asked, "You mean to tell me that the hole in the center of your ant hill goes all the way to China?"

"Sure does," was her reply.

"No way," said Buck again.

"Way," the Queen said again.

"Oh my gosh," said Buck trying to catch his breath. "How did you ever do it?"

"It wasn't easy," replied Queen Sharmain. "Our drilling team missed China on our first dig. They hit the middle of Australia, popped out, got scared by the kangaroos and the anteaters, backed up and re-drilled."

"They hit all kinds of stuff going down—rock, clay, underground water streams, veins of gold, silver, coal—all kinds of stuff. It was a geologist's dream come true. Once they hit the center they couldn't go down anymore and had to start digging up again. I heard it was quite a mess, but they did it. They dug all the way through to China and came up right next to the Great Wall of China in the middle of a tourist picnic area... and wow, were the Chinese people ever surprised. They were awesome, friendly, and wanted to know everything about us ants and where we came from. They couldn't believe we came from the other side of the world."

"We were even in the newspaper, but we couldn't understand what they wrote because we can't read Chinese. We immediately set up a free trade agreement. They wanted all the American food we could supply—potato chips, hot dogs, hamburgers, candy apples, fudge—you know, all the stuff we usually pick up at our picnic ground. In exchange we get the most delicious Chinese food—egg foo young, fried rice, and a Mongolian stir-fry that will make you smile all night long! Come on over to the ant hill and try some. The Chinese egg rolls are outstanding. We have plenty to share.

We've been stocking up for over a month now! We are going to have a Chinese winter!"

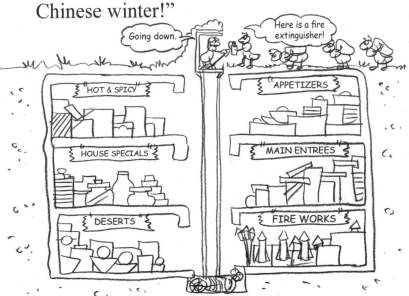

CHAPTER 11

WHAT DO WE DO?

"Thanks, Queen Sharmain. Save us some for later. We first have a little bit of a problem we need to deal with and I think you can help."

"I understand. Deelores flew me around our ant hill. I had no idea how big of a hill we made, or the mess we made. I didn't know we were blocking the animal trail crossroads. We got so involved in what we were doing that we didn't pay attention to what was going on around us. That was selfish of us and not the right thing to do. We will get this straightened out immediately. My ants can do almost anything they put their minds to, and if I ask them they will do almost anything for me…just like they dug to China!"

"Good," said Buck. "If we could only move that ant hill a little into the woods. We wouldn't have to move it far, just off of the main trails and then you wouldn't bother anything. You don't have to do all the work yourselves. We can pitch in and all help. The more of us that work, the faster it will go—and it might be fun too!"

"Okay," said Queen Sharmain. "Let's give it a try, but before we go, may I have a little more biscuit and honey? Maybe in a carry-out bag?"

"Me too, please," said Rascal.

"My pleasure," said Buck.

CHAPTER 12

EVERYONE PITCHES IN

Deelores gave Queen Sharmain and her six ant guards a ride back to their ant hill. Dee flew a couple of extra loops and dips, just for the excitement of it. You should of heard the ant guards screaming, "Hold on!" Queen Sharmain loved it. Maury and Rascal went out into the woods and along the trails and spread the word that help was needed to

move the giant ant hill. The very next morning, right at daybreak, when the black and white of night leaves and the color of the day starts to show, all kinds of forest animals were there to help.

The beavers pushed dirt with their tails, the moose and deer with their antlers, the rabbits with their feet, and even Buck was there shoveling.

83

With all of the help combined and with the ants' teamwork they had that giant hill moved by the end of the day. The animal trails and the big crossroads were open once again and life in the woods soon went back to normal. Maury again visited his mother and she was happy to see him. All the animals passed each other on the trails with a big smile and a thumbs-up.

The ants apologized to all the animals in the woods and one night put on a Chinese fireworks display that lit up the night sky for hours.

Queen Sharmain soon had her appetite full of Chinese food and found that it tasted better if only eaten once in a while. The ants closed the hole to China and went back to raiding the picnic area.

Rascal went back to taking long naps in the tree house, catching the fish in the aquarium, and helping Buck with household chores. Buck always kept a clean house and expected Rascal to always do his share. Rascal loved being in the tree house and never minded when Buck would ask him to do helpful chores.

Buck also settled back into his normal way of life. He would take long walks in the woods, sometimes he would fish late at night and watch for shooting stars. He always enjoyed writing stories about what he saw and learned.

THE END

His next story is about something he saw happening in the woods. It was the time the owls decided not to give a hoot anymore and what Buck had to do to help. We will see you in Buck Wilder's next exciting adventure story and you will find out why the 'Owls Didn't Give a Hoot!'

See you there!

91

SECRET MESSAGE DECODING PAGE

Hidden in this book is a secret Buck Wilder message. You need to figure it out. Hidden in many of the drawings are letters that, when put together, make up a statement, a Buck Wilder statement. Your job is to find those letters and always remember the message – it's important.

DO NOT write in this book if it's from the library, your classroom, or borrowed from someone.

If you need help finding the hidden letters turn the page.

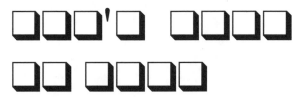

14 letters make up 4 words.

The secret letters are hidden on the following pages in this order...

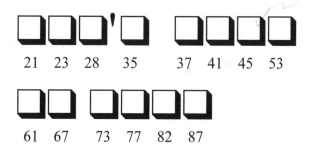

☐	☐	☐	'	☐		☐	☐	☐	☐
21	23	28		35		37	41	45	53

☐	☐		☐	☐	☐	☐
61	67		73	77	82	87

14 letters make up 4 words.

Remember – Don't Write in this Book!

95

Mackinac Island Press

for the love of reading